W9-AWY-931

PRAYERS OF THE SAINTS

ALSO BY WOODEENE KOENIG-BRICKER

*365 Saints: Your Daily Guide
to the Wisdom and Wonder of Their Lives*

PRAYERS
OF THE
SAINTS

An Inspired Collection
of Holy Wisdom

WOODEENE KOENIG-BRICKER

HarperSanFrancisco
An Imprint of HarperCollins*Publishers*

PRAYERS OF THE SAINTS: *An Inspired Collection of Holy Wisdom.* Copyright © 1996 by Woodeene Koenig-Bricker. All rights reserved. Printed in the United States of America. No part of this book may be used or reproduced in any manner whatsoever without written permission except in the case of brief quotations embodied in critical articles and reviews. For information address HarperCollins Publishers, 10 East 53rd Street, New York, NY 10022.

HarperCollins Web Site: http://www.harpercollins.com

HarperCollins®, 🏛®, and HarperSanFrancisco™ are trademarks of HarperCollins Publishers Inc.

Book design by Claudia Smelser
Set in Aldus and Trajan

FIRST EDITION

Library of Congress Cataloging-in-Publication Data
Koenig-Bricker, Woodeene.
    Prayers of the saints : an inspired collection of holy wisdom / Woodeene Koenig-Bricker — 1st ed.
    ISBN 0–06–064782—5 (pbk.)
    1. Prayers.   2. Christian saints.   3. Christian saints—Biography. I. Title.
BV245.K64   1996
242'.8—dc20   96–11287

96 97 98 99 00 ❖ HAD 10 9 8 7 6 5 4 3 2 1

To my mother . . .

who taught me how to pray
by praying with the saints

ACKNOWLEDGMENTS

MY THANKS to all who have helped me with this project, especially to

John and Matthew, without whose love I would have never tried.

The many friars of the Western Province of the Order of Preachers, who helped with translations, advice, and hospitality.

Bob Lockwood and Greg Erlandson, who could have said "no" but instead said "go for it!"

Bert Ghezzi, who had faith in me even when I didn't have faith in myself.

All those spoken and unspoken in my heart whose encouragement kept me going.

❧

Grateful acknowledgment is made for permission to reprint excerpts from the following works.

St. Dimitrii of Rostov reprinted from *The Orthodox Way* by Bishop Kallistos Ware. Copyright © 1979 St. Vladimir's Orthodox Theological Seminary, Crestwood, NY.

Gertrude of Helfta reprinted from *Gertrude of Helfta* translated by Margaret Winkworth. Copyright © 1993 Paulist Press.

St. Anthony Mary Claret reprinted from *St. Anthony Mary Claret Autobiography* edited by José Maria Vinas, C.M.F. Copyright © 1976 Claretian Publications.

St. Maximillian Kolbe reprinted from *Stronger Than Hatred, A Collection of Spiritual Writings.* Copyright © 1988 New City Press.

St. Elizabeth Ann Seton reprinted from *Elizabeth Seton, An American Woman* by Leonard Feeney. Copyright © 1975 Our Sunday Visitor Inc.

St. Ignatius Loyola reprinted from *Traditional Catholic Prayers,* edited by Msgr. Charles J. Dolen. Copyright © Our Sunday Visitor Inc.

St. Clare reprinted from *Traditional Catholic Prayers,* edited by Msgr. Charles J. Dolen. Copyright © Our Sunday Visitor Inc.

St. Benedict of Nursia reprinted from *Traditional Catholic Prayers,* edited by Msgr. Charles J. Dolen. Copyright © Our Sunday Visitor Inc.

St. Catherine of Siena reprinted from *Traditional Catholic Prayers,* edited by Msgr. Charles J. Dolen. Copyright © Our Sunday Visitor Inc.

St. Alphonsus Liguori reprinted from *Traditional Catholic Prayers*, edited by Msgr. Charles J. Dolen. Copyright © Our Sunday Visitor Inc.

St. Anselm of Canterbury reprinted from *Traditional Catholic Prayers*, edited by Msgr. Charles J. Dolen. Copyright © Our Sunday Visitor Inc.

St. Thomas More reprinted from *Traditional Catholic Prayers*, edited by Msgr. Charles J. Dolen. Copyright © Our Sunday Visitor Inc.

Thomas á Kempis reprinted from *Traditional Catholic Prayers*, edited by Msgr. Charles J. Dolen. Copyright © Our Sunday Visitor Inc.

St. Margaret Mary Alacoque reprinted from *Traditional Catholic Prayers*, edited by Msgr. Charles J. Dolen. Copyright © Our Sunday Visitor Inc.

St. Bernard reprinted from *Traditional Catholic Prayers*, edited by Msgr. Charles J. Dolen. Copyright © Our Sunday Visitor Inc.

St. Mary Magdalen dei Pazzi reprinted from *Traditional Catholic Prayers*, edited by Msgr. Charles J. Dolen. Copyright © Our Sunday Visitor Inc.

St. Edmund reprinted from *Traditional Catholic Prayers*, edited by Msgr. Charles J. Dolen. Copyright © Our Sunday Visitor Inc.

St. Symeon the New Theologian reprinted from *Hymns of Divine Love* by St. Symeon the New Theologian introduction and translation by George A. Maloney, S.J. Copyright © 1978 Dimension Books Inc, Denville, N.J.

St. Don Bosco reprinted from *A Spiritual Portrait* by Edna Beyer Phelan. Copyright © 1963 Doubleday & Company.

St. John of the Cross translated by Fred Lucci, O.P.

St. Thomas Aquinas translated by Augustine Thompson, O.P.

St. Catherine dei Ricci translated by Augustine Thompson, O.P.

Bl. Jordan of Saxony, O.P. to St. Dominic translated by Augustine Thompson, O.P.

Catherine of Siena from *The Communion of Saints: Prayers of the Famous*. Copyright © 1990 by Wm B. Eerdmans Publishing Co.

St. Anselm from *The Prayers and Meditations of St. Anselm*, translated by Sister Benedicta Ward, S.L.G. Copyright © 1973 Penguin Books.

St. Clement of Rome from *Early Christian Writings, the Apostolic Fathers*, translated by Maxwell Staniforth. Copyright © 1973 Penguin Books.

Hildegard of Bingen from *Medieval Women's Visionary Literature* edited by Elizabeth Alvilda Petroff. Copyright © 1986 Petroff.

INTRODUCTION

I'VE COLLECTED PRAYERS of the saints for years. Torn from the backs of church bulletins, copied from old novena and Mass cards, jotted in my notebook, they have been part of my personal "prayer book" for years, but I never expected to do much more with them than contemplate memorizing a few now and then. When the opportunity came to share some of my favorite prayers of the saints—and to find some new ones as well—I was delighted. This collection is the result.

There is a saying in theology: *lex orendi, lex credendi.* Loosely translated, it means that what you say when you pray is what you believe. If that's so, then the prayers in this collection probably reflect as much of my own theology as they do that of the saints, for the major criterion for inclusion was simply that I had to like the prayer.

Since I prefer the plain to the flowery, the clear to the obscure, the straightforward to the enigmatic, the prayers in this collection tend to be plain, clear, and straightforward. But every now and then I've been enchanted with a distinctive turn of phrase, such as Saint Gregory's prayer that begins "Alas, dear Christ, the Dragon is here again," Saint John of the Cross's haunting line "If only I could die because then I would not die," or Saint Augustine's exquisite "Too late I have loved you, O Beauty of ancient days, yet ever new?" The result is, I hope, a mixture of prayers that will reflect the reader's various moods and needs, as much as they reflect my moods and needs.

Many of the prayers here are quite short, sometimes because they were recorded on the saint's deathbed and deathbed sayings tend to be brief. But more often they are concise because our deepest and most heartfelt prayers tend to be succinct. The brevity of these prayers can be a benefit, because they are short enough to be easily memorized and carried in our hearts.

Certainly the prayers in this collection do not represent all the prayers of the saints, or perhaps not even their best prayers. All the saints have gone to Mass and joined in the prayers of the Eucharist. Many have said the traditional prayers of the church such as the Liturgy of the Hours and the rosary. Moreover, it is entirely possible that the greatest pray-ers among the saints never wrote their words down for posterity—or they might never have been heard to say them aloud by followers who recorded them.

For each prayer included here, I have attempted to ascertain that the saint actually said the words, or at least a close approximation of them. That's why I have not included the famous prayer attributed to Saint Francis that begins "Make me an instrument of your peace." Scholars now agree Francis never penned those words; they were, in fact, written by an Anglican clergyman.

One other aspect of these prayers is they are all apparently addressed to God. While many saints had a great devotion to the Blessed Virgin Mary and wrote eloquent prayers praising her and asking for her intercession, I choose not to include those because they represent a particular form of piety that is not universal. However, prayers to the triune God of Christianity—Father, Son, and Holy Spirit—are an essential aspect of every saint's spiritual journey of faith.

I hope you will find at least one or two prayers that will resonate within your soul and accompany you on your own journey.

I am sometimes asked which prayer is my favorite. While I like all the prayers, one I say often in times of stress is Julian of Norwich's "All shall be well and all shall be well and all manner of thing shall be well." It never fails to bring me comfort and consolation. May you, too, discover that in the words of the saints, all *shall* be well.

PRAYERS OF THE SAINTS

MARY, MOTHER OF JESUS

FIRST CENTURY A.D.

U PON *being asked by the angel Gabriel to become the mother of Jesus, Mary, a young
peasant woman from Nazareth, answered
in the words that have become known*
throughout Christendom as the Magnificat.

My being proclaims the greatness of the Lord,
my spirit finds joy in God my savior.
For he has looked upon his servant in her lowliness;
all ages to come shall call me blessed.
God who is mighty has done great things for me,
holy is his name;
His mercy is from age to age
on those who fear him.
He has shown might with his arm;
he has confused the proud in their inmost thoughts.
He has deposed the mighty from their thrones
and raised the lowly to high places.

The hungry he has given every good thing,
while the rich he has sent empty away.
He has upheld Israel his servant,
ever mindful of his mercy
Even as he promised our fathers,
promised Abraham and his descendants forever.

(Lk. 1: 46–55)

SAINT PATRICK

389–461?

ALTHOUGH *he is inexorably associated with Ireland, by birth Saint Patrick was a Roman of British origin. When he was about fourteen, he was captured by raiders and shipped to Ireland as a slave. Although he eventually escaped, he returned several years later to spread the message of Christ to the Irish. Composed at a time when few people could read and write, his prayer, "The Breastplate of Saint Patrick," reflects his desire to become a living Gospel to all he encountered.*

THE BREASTPLATE OF SAINT PATRICK

Christ be with me, Christ before me, Christ behind
  me,
Christ in me, Christ beneath me, Christ above me,
Christ on my right, Christ on my left,
Christ where I lie, Christ where I sit, Christ where
  I arise,

Christ in the heart of every one who thinks of me,
Christ in the mouth of every one who speaks of me,
Christ in every eye that sees me,
Christ in every ear that hears me.
Salvation is of the Lord.
Salvation is of the Lord,
Salvation is of the Christ.
May your salvation Lord, be ever with us.

SAINT RICHARD OF CHICHESTER

1197–1253

FALLING *under the wrath of King Henry III, who wanted one of his own toadies elevated to the position of Bishop of Chichester, Saint Richard was reduced to a virtual outcast in his own diocese. He might have become bitter and angry, but, as his famous prayer demonstrates, he refused to focus on his misfortune, concentrating always on his gratitude.*

Thank you, Lord Jesus Christ,
For all the benefits and blessings
which you have given me,
For all the pains and insults
which you have borne for me.
Merciful Friend, Brother and Redeemer,
May I know you more clearly,
Love you more dearly,
And follow you more nearly,
Day by day.

BLESSED JULIAN OF NORWICH

1343–1423

ONE OF *the most beloved mystics of all time, Blessed Julian might sound in the following prayer as if she were an incurable optimist. On the contrary, at times in her life Julian was so unhappy and despairing that she prayed for an early death. Knowing that she experienced such intense anguish and depression makes her succinct and heartfelt prayer all the more poignant.*

All shall be well
and all shall be well
and all manner of thing shall be well.

SAINT AUGUSTINE

354–430

S AINT AUGUSTINE *was raised by a Christian mother, but according to the custom of his time, he put off baptism. In the meantime, he studied philosophy, took a mistress by whom he had a son, opened a school of rhetoric, and, in general, led a pleasant and well-satisfied life. Although he gradually became convinced of the truth of Christianity, he was reluctant to convert, praying at one time, "Give me chastity, but not yet." Finally, at age thirty-two, he agreed to be baptized by Saint Ambrose. His prayers reveal one of the most literate saints the church has ever known.*

Too late I have loved you, O Beauty of ancient days, yet ever new? Too late I have loved you! And behold, you were within, and I abroad, and there I searched for you; I was deformed, plunging amid those fair forms, which you had made. You were with me, but I was not with you. Things held me far from you—things which, if they were not in you, were not at all. You called, and shouted, and burst my deafness. You flashed and shone, and scattered my blindness. You breathed odors and I drew in breath—and I pant for you. I tasted, and I hunger and I thirst. You touched me, and I burned for your peace.

O God, by whose laws the poles revolve, the stars follow their courses, the sun rules the day and the moon presides over the night; and all the world maintains, as far as this world of sense allows, the wondrous stability of things by means of the orders and recurrences of seasons: through the days by the changing of light and darkness, through the months by the moon's progressions and declines, through the years by the successions of Spring, Summer, Autumn and Winter, through the cycles by the completion of the sun's course, through the great eras of time by the return of the stars to their starting points.

God of life, there are days when the burdens we carry chafe our shoulders and wear us down; when the road seems dreary and endless, the skies gray and threatening; when our lives have no music in them and our hearts are lonely, and our souls have lost their courage. Flood the path with light, we beseech you; turn our eyes to where the skies are full of promise.

Our hearts are restless, O Lord, until they rest in you.

SAINT IGNATIUS OF LOYOLA

1491–1556

THE FOUNDER *of the Jesuits, Saint Ignatius of Loyola intended to become a soldier until a cannonball shattered both his leg and his dreams of an illustrious army career. A man of great determination and self-control (he had his broken leg rebroken and reset not once but twice, without benefit of anesthesia!), Saint Ignatius's straightforward, almost militaristic style is evident in his forthright prayers.*

Receive, Lord, all my liberty, my memory, my understanding and my whole will. You have given me all that I have, all that I am, and I surrender all to your divine will, that you dispose of me. Give me only your love and your grace. With this I am rich enough, and have no more to ask.

Dearest Lord,
teach me to be generous.
Teach me to serve you as you deserve;

to give and not to count the cost;
to fight, and not to heed the wounds;
to labor, and not to seek to rest;
to give of myself and not to ask for reward,
except the reward of knowing that I am doing
    your will.

SAINT JOHN OF DAMASCUS

A.D. 749

ONE OF *the greatest poets of the Eastern church, Saint John of Damascus entered the monastery of Saint Sabas with his adopted brother Cosmas. The two spent their spare time composing and singing hymns, much to the chagrin of their fellow monks, who thought such activity was frivolous and scandalous. Fortunately for us, some of Saint John's greatest hymns of praise were saved to resound through the centuries.*

> O Day of Resurrection!
> Let us beam with festive joy!
> Today indeed is the Lord's own Passover,
> For from death to life, from earth to heaven
> Christ has led us
> As we shout the victory hymn!
> Christ has risen from the dead!

SAINT CLARE

1193–1253

F ROM *the moment she first heard Saint Francis of Assisi speak, Saint Clare was determined to follow his way of life. Sneaking away from her friends and family, she met Francis and his monks* in secret, cut her hair, and put on the habit of the Franciscans. Although her family tried to force her to return home, she persisted in her resolve and was eventually joined by her mother and sister. Her prayers, like those of her mentor, Francis, are filled with joy at the goodness of the Lord.

Go forth in peace, for you have followed the good road. Go forth without fear, for he who created you has made you holy, has always protected you, and loves you as a mother. Blessed be you, my God, for having created me.

Praise and glory to you, O loving Jesus Christ,
for the most sacred wound in your side,

and by that adorable wound and by your infinite
     mercy
which you made known to us in the opening of
     your breast to the soldier Longinus,
and so to us all.
I pray you, O most gentle Jesus,
having redeemed me by baptism from original sin,
so now, by your Precious Blood, which is offered
     and received throughout the world,
deliver me from all evils, past, present and to come.
And, by your most bitter death,
give me a lively faith, a firm hope, and a perfect
     charity,
so that I may love you with all my heart, all my
     soul, and all my strength;
make me firm and steadfast in good works and
     grant me perseverance in your service
so that I may be able to please you always.

SAINT TERESA OF AVILA

1515–1582

CHARMING, *witty, determined, candid, out-spoken, passionate—these are but a few of the adjectives applied to Saint Teresa of Avila. One of only two women named Doc-*tors of the Church (Catherine of Siena is the other), *Saint Teresa experienced mystical visions and miracu-lous events, but she also talked with God in an almost conversational tone, frankly speaking her mind on a variety of topics. Her "Bookmark" is one of the most famous prayers ever written.*

From silly devotions and sullen saints, deliver me, O Lord.

❧

Govern all by your wisdom, O Lord, so that my soul may always be serving you as you will and not as I choose. Do not punish me, I beseech, by granting that which I wish or ask, if it offend your love which would always live in me. Let me die to myself that I may serve

you. Let me live to you who in yourself are the true
life.

BOOKMARK OF SAINT TERESA OF AVILA

Let nothing disturb you
nothing frighten you,
all things are passing;
Patient endurance
attains all things:
one whom God possesses
wants nothing
for God alone suffices.

SAINT THÉRÈSE OF LISIEUX

1873–1897

THE LITTLE FLOWER, *as she is often called, Saint Thérèse of Lisieux became a saint not by performing great miracles but by doing little things with great love—putting up with frustrating companions, obeying superiors, finishing the laundry. So ordinary did she appear, some of the sisters in her convent were unaware of her remarkable prayer life until after her death.*

My life is an instant,
a fleeting hour.
My life is a moment,
which swiftly escapes me.
O my God, you know that
on earth I have only today
to love you.

O my divine Master! I cried from the bottom of my heart, is it Your justice alone that will receive victims of holocausts? Has not also Your merciful love need of them? Everywhere it is misunderstood, rejected. . . . The hearts upon which You long so generously to bestow it, turn aside to creatures and, for the miserable pleasure of an instant, ask happiness from them, instead of throwing themselves into Your arms and accepting the sweet torrent of Your infinite love.

❧

Your face is the only fatherland for me.

SAINT FRANCIS OF ASSISI

1181?–1226

PERHAPS *the most famous of all saints, Saint Francis of Assisi recognized God in all creation. The following excerpt from his famous "Canticle of the Sun," written while he was suffering great agony prior to his death, gives thanks for the entire universe, especially for Sister Death, whose arrival Francis was anxiously waiting.*

CANTICLE OF THE SUN

O most high, almighty Lord God, to you belong
praise, glory, honor and all blessing!
Praised be You my Lord God, with all your
creatures, especially Brother Sun, who brings us
the day and who brings us the light; fair is he
and shines with great splendor.
O Lord, he signifies You to us!
Praised be You, my Lord, for Sister Moon and for
the stars, clear and lovely in the heavens

Praised be You, my Lord, for our brother the wind,
and for air and cloud, calms and all weather by
which you uphold life in all creatures.
Praised be You, my Lord, for Brother Fire, through
whom you light the night. He is beautiful and
playful and robust and strong . . .
Praised be You, my Lord, for our Sister Bodily
Death, from whom no one escapes . . .

We adore you and we bless you, Lord Jesus Christ, here
and in all churches which are in the whole world, because by your holy cross you have redeemed the world.

SAINT IGNATIUS OF ANTIOCH

C. A.D. 107

AFTER *having been condemned by the Emperor Trajan to die in the public games, Saint Ignatius, Bishop of Antioch, was hauled to Rome in the back of a cart. Along the way, he prayed that he would not inconvenience anyone who might want to rescue his body. Apparently his prayer was answered, for tradition says he was completely devoured by the lions as soon as he was thrown into the arena.*

Let me be food for wild beasts, for they are my way to God. I am Jesus Christ's wheat. I must therefore be ground and broken by the teeth of wild beasts that I may become His pure and spotless bread. . . . I desire and pray that the animals will not leave anything of me on the earth and that, when my spirit has flown to eternal rest, my body may not be an inconvenience to anyone.

Receive in tranquility and peace, O Lord, the souls of your servants who have departed this present life to come to you. Grant them rest and place them in the habitations of light, the abodes of blessed spirits. Give them the life that will not age, good things that will not pass away, delights that have no end, through Jesus Christ our Lord.

SAINT HILARY OF POITIERS

C. A.D. 368

S AINT JEROME *calls Saint Hilary a "most eloquent man" and complains that he uses long, involved sentences in his dissertations. Yet this prayer of Saint Hilary, who spent much of his life condemning a heresy that denied the divinity of Jesus, demonstrates his ability to state his position without wasting words.*

O Lord, keep us from vain strife of words:
Grant to us a constant
Profession of the Truth.
Preserve us in the Faith,
True Faith and undefiled,
That ever we may hold fast
That which we professed when we were Baptized
Unto, and in the Name of the
Father, Son and the Holy Ghost

SAINT BENEDICT

480?–547

*S*AINT BENEDICT *is often called "The Father of Western Monasticism," and rightly so. He built twelve monasteries during his lifetime, and even today many religious orders follow the rule or canon that he set down for his monks. His prayers, like his rule, clearly and unabashedly set forth the Christian way of life.*

O Lord,
I place myself in your hands and dedicate myself to
 you.
I pledge myself to do your will in all things—
To love the Lord God with all my heart, all my soul,
 all my strength.
Not to kill, not to steal, not to covet, not to bear
 false witness,
to honor all persons.

Not to do to another what I should not want done
   to myself.
To chastise the body.
Not to seek after pleasures. To love fasting. To
   relieve the poor.
To clothe the naked. To visit the sick. To bury the
   dead.
To help in trouble. To console the sorrowing.
To hold myself aloof from worldly ways.
To prefer nothing to the love of Christ.
Not to give way to anger.
Not to foster a desire for revenge.
Not to entertain deceit in the heart.
Not to make a false peace. Not to forsake charity.
Not to swear, lest I swear falsely.
To speak the truth with heart and tongue

Not to return evil for evil.
To do no injury, indeed, even to bear patiently any
injury done to me.
To love my enemies.
Not to curse those who curse me
but rather to bless them.
To bear persecution for justice's sake.
Not to be proud.
Not to be given to intoxicating drink.
Not to be an overeater.
Not to be lazy.
Not to be slothful.
Not to be a murmurer.
Not to be a detractor.
To put my trust in God.
To refer the good I see in myself to God.
To refer any evil I see in myself to myself.
To fear the day of judgment.
To be in dread of hell.
To desire eternal life with spiritual longing.

To keep death before my eyes daily.

To keep constant watch over my actions.

To remember that God sees me everywhere.

To call upon Christ for defense against evil
thoughts that arise in my heart.

To guard my tongue against wicked speech.

To avoid much speaking.

To avoid idle talk.

Not to seek to appear clever.

To read only what is good to read.

To pray often.

To ask forgiveness daily for my sins, and to seek
ways to amend my life.

To obey my superiors in all things rightful.

Not to desire to be thought holy, but to seek
holiness.

To fulfill the commandments of God by good works.

To love chastity.

To hate no one.

Not be jealous or envious of anyone.

Not to love strife.

Not to love pride.

To honor the aged.

To pray for my enemies.

To make peace after a quarrel, before the setting of
the sun.

Never to despair of your mercy, O God of Mercy.

❧

Grant O Gracious

O Holy Father

Upon me to bestow:

Intellect to understand You

Perceptions to perceive You

Reason to discern You

Diligence to seek You

Wisdom to find You

A spirit to know You

SAINT ANTHONY OF PADUA

1195–1231

FOR MANY *Catholic Christians, Saint Anthony of Padua is the saint to invoke to find lost items. The son of Portuguese nobility, Saint Anthony first joined the Augustinians, but when the relics of some Franciscan martyrs were brought through his town, he entered their order. Loved in his lifetime as a preacher and teacher, he is the patron saint of animals as well as lost objects.*

Lord Jesus, bind us to you and to our neighbor with
love.
May our hearts not be turned away from you.
May our souls not be deceived nor our talents or
minds enticed by allurements of error, so that we
may never distance ourselves from your love.
Thus may we love our neighbor as ourselves with
strength, wisdom and gentleness. With your
help, you who are blessed throughout all ages.

Behold the Cross of the Lord!
Begone you enemy powers!
The Lion of the Tribe of Judah
The Root of David, has conquered.
Alleluia

SAINT JOHN VIANNEY,
THE CURÉ OF ARS

1786–1859

S AINT JOHN VIANNEY, *the parish priest in the village of Ars, France, was a man of simple means and simple tastes. Humble and modest, he possessed remarkable common sense. His approach to holiness reflected his simple, homespun attitude toward life, yet stories of his miracles, especially the ability to recognize secret sin, continue to be told. His prayer is indicative of his down-to-earth holiness.*

O my God, come to me, so that You may dwell in
me and I may dwell in you.

SAINT CLOTILDA

A.D. 545

WHAT *greater loss can a parent suffer than the death of a child? Saint Clotilda's prayer at the death of her firstborn son encompasses both her faith and her anguish. But her sorrows were only beginning. Her other sons grew up to become embroiled in war and fratricide. It was only through her earnest prayers at the shrine of Saint Martin that her last two did not kill each other in battle.*

I give thanks to Almighty God that He has not considered me unworthy to be the mother of a child admitted into the celestial kingdom. Having quitted the word in the white robe of his innocence, he will rejoice in the presence of God through all eternity.

SAINT ELIZABETH ANN SETON

1774–1821

THE FIRST *saint born in the United States, Elizabeth Ann Seton was first and foremost a wife and mother. When her beloved husband died after an extended illness, she devoted herself to her five children, studiously caring for them even after she had founded her religious order, the American Sisters of Charity. Her prayers reveal the sorrow that never completely left her heart.*

Eternity, eternity, when shall I come to You at last? . . . in eternity where we will love with a glance of the soul.

❦

Almighty and Giver of all mercies, Father of all, who knows my heart and pities its weaknesses: You know the desire of my soul to do Your will. It struggles to wing its flight to You its Creator and sinks again in sorrow for that imperfection which draws it back to earth. How long will I contend with sin and morality. . .

Redeemer of sinners! Who gave Your life to save us, assist a miserable sinner who strives with the corruption and desires above all things to break the snares of the enemy.

SAINT GEMMA GALGANI

1878–1903

A WOMAN *of enormous physical as well as spiritual beauty, Saint Gemma Galgani lived a life of piety, charity, and suffering. Although she desired to become a Passionist nun, her frail health prevented her from joining the convent. Her passion for Christ as well as her pain are reflected in her prayers.*

Jesus, destroy this chain of a body, for I shall never be content until my soul can fly to you. When shall I be completely blessed in you?

If I saw the gates of Hell open and I stood on the brink of the abyss, I should not despair, I should not lose hope of mercy, because I should trust in You, my God.

My Jesus, I struggle . . . I die . . . I die because of You. Jesus, Lord of strong souls, strengthen me, purify me, make me divine. Great God, God of every sacrifice, Jesus, help me; my Redemption, God from God, come to my aid. Continually You watch over me. I thirst for You, Jesus. Do You not see how I suffer in the morning before you come to me . . . You, Jesus, are the flame of my heart. My Jesus, I would love You with my whole being. All you saints in heaven, lend me your hearts.

SAINT MARGARET OF CORTONA

1247–1297

HER EARLY *hagiographies say Margaret of Cortona led "an irregular life." She was, in fact, a wealthy man's mistress until his murder. Her change in attitude, as well as her contrition after his death, has led her to be called "the perfect penitent." She spent the rest of her life working on behalf of the poor and making reparation for her sins.*

This morning my soul is greater than the world since it possesses You, You whom heaven and earth do not contain.—said after Holy Communion

SAINT VINCENT PALLOTTI

1795–1850

S AINT VINCENT PALLOTTI, *the son of a Roman grocer, devoted his entire life to helping ordinary people grow in holiness. To that end, he organized schools for shoemakers, joiners, gardeners, tailors, coachmen, and young workers, saying "Holiness is simply to do God's will, always and everywhere."*

Not the intellect, but God;
not the will, but God;
not the soul, but God; . . .
not taste, but God; . . .
not touch, but God; . . .
not the heart, but God;
not the body, but God; . . .
not food and drink, but God;
not clothing, but God;

not repose in bed, but God; . . .
not riches, but God;
not distinctions, but God . . .
God in all and always.

SAINT GERTRUDE THE GREAT

1256–1301

SAINT GERTRUDE *was left by her parents at the fa-mous convent at Helfta when she was about five years old. Growing up under the charge of Saint Mechtildis, she probably never left the cloister. Her fame has increased in recent years because of her "Reve-lations," which recount a series of her visions and mysti-cal experiences. Her prayers, however, reflect a woman as well grounded in the practical as in the mystical.*

How I wish, O Lord, that my soul might burn with such a fire that it might melt and be like some liquid sub-stance so that it could be entirely poured out into you!

❧

I vow obedience to You because Your fatherly charity allures me, Your loving kindness and gentleness attract me. In observing Your will, I tie myself to you because clinging to you is lovable above everything.

SAINT CATHERINE OF SIENA

1347–1380

EVEN IF *she had never become one of the Church's greatest saints, Catherine of Siena would be remarkable for having had the courage to upbraid the Pope about his shortcomings. The youngest of twenty-five children, she is one of only two women named a Doctor of the Church. Her "Dialogue of Saint Catherine" is one of the great mystical treasures of the Middle Ages, and her prayers reveal her deep passion and strength of character.*

O abyss, O eternal Godhead, O sea profound, what more could you give me than yourself? You are the fire that ever burns without being consumed; you consume in your heat all the soul's self-love; you are the fire which takes away cold; with your light you illuminate me so that I may know all your truth. Clothe me, clothe me with your eternal truth, so that I may run this mortal life with true obedience and with the light of your most holy faith.

O tender Father, you gave me more, much more than I ever thought to ask for.

I realize that our human desires can never really match what you long to give us.

Thanks and again thanks, O Father, for having granted my petitions, and that which I never realized I needed or petitioned.

SAINT COLUMBA OF IONA

521?–597

O NE OF *the most beloved Scottish saints, Saint Columba was a scholar by nature. Inordinately fond of books, he even got into a lawsuit with Saint Finnian over a copy of Saint Jerome's psalter. While gentleness was never one of his virtues, he is said to have mellowed in his old age, praying simply that he be allowed a "door in paradise."*

Almighty Father, Son and Holy Ghost, eternal everblessed gracious God; to me the least of saints, to me allow that I may keep a door in paradise. That I may keep even the smallest door, the furthest, the darkest, coldest door, the door that is least used, the stiffest door. If so it be but in your house, O God, if it so be that I can see your glory even afar, and hear your voice, O God, and know that I am with you, O God.

SAINT DOMINIC

1170–1221

THE FOUNDER *of the Order of Preachers, Saint Dominic has never been as well known as his contemporary, Saint Francis of Assisi. Yet Dominic's order has produced some of the greatest saints in the history of Christianity, including Catherine of Siena, Albert the Great, Thomas Aquinas, Rose of Lima, and Martin de Porres, to mention but a few. In this prayer attributed to him, Saint Dominic emphasizes the importance of preaching the Gospel; even today his followers take that message to heart.*

May God the Father who made us bless us
May God the Son send his healing among us
May God the Holy Spirit move within us and
    give us
eyes to see with, ears to hear with and hands
that your work might be done.

May we walk and preach the word of God to all.
May the angel of peace watch over us and lead us
   at last
by God's grace to the Kingdom.

SAINT THERESA MARGARET
OF THE SACRED HEART

1748–1770

A T AGE *seventeen Anna Maria Redi entered the Carmelite convent of Saint Teresa in Florence, Italy. As Saint Theresa Margaret of the Sacred Heart, she spent five years giving herself to Christ in prayer and ministering to her fellow sisters. Her prayer is as beautiful as it is simple.*

I want to love you, O my God, with a love that is patient, with a love that abandons itself wholly to you, with a love that acts, and most important of all, with a love that perseveres.

VENERABLE CHARLES DE FOUCAULD

1858–1916

CHARLES DE FOUCAULD, *better known as Little Brother Charles of Jesus, spent the first part of his life living fast and free. The remaining part he spent as a hermit in the Algerian desert, where he came to understand that although self-discipline is necessary for holiness, such discipline is not possible without the help of God.*

Father, I abandon myself into Your hands;
do with me what You will.
Whatever You may do, I thank You;
I am ready for all, I accept all.
Let only Your will be done in me,
and in all Your creatures—
I wish no more than this, O Lord.
Into Your hands I commend my soul;
I offer it to You with all the love of my heart,
For I love You, Lord!

And so need to give myself,
surrender myself into Your hands,
without reserve,
and with boundless confidence,
For You are my Father.

SAINT SYMEON
THE NEW THEOLOGIAN

949–1022

THE GREATEST *of the Byzantine mystical writers, Saint Symeon lyrically expressed his faith, even when he was forced into exile in Asia Minor. His prayer asks the timeless questions put forth by all who struggle to know God.*

How are You at once the source of fire,
how also the fountain of dew?
How at once burning and sweetness,
how a remedy for all corruption?
How do You make gods of us men,
how do You make darkness light?
How do You make one reascend from Hell,
how do You make us mortals imperishable?
How do You draw darkness to light,
how do You triumph over night?
How do You illumine the heart,

how do You transform me entirely?
How do You become one with men,
how do You make them sons of God?
How do You burn them with Your love,
how do You wound them without a sword?
How can You be patient, how can You endure?
How do You not remunerate at once?
How do You see the actions of all,
You who dwell beyond all creatures?
How do You look at the conduct of each one,
You, who are so far from us?
Give patience to Your servants,
so that trials may not overwhelm them!

SAINT PRISCA

FIRST CENTURY A.D.

W HILE *little is know about Saint Prisca, we do know that she was but one of many courageous men and women who were willing to suffer death during the persecutions of* ancient Rome rather than worship a false god. Her prayer, said just before her execution, is a reflection of her immortal faith and her all-too-mortal fear.

O Lord God, Eternal King! You who stretched out the heavens and built the earth. You who put limits on the ocean and trampled the Serpent's head. You, O Lord, do not abandon me now. Hear my prayer.

BLESSED ROSE HAWTHORNE LATHROP

1851–1926

NOT ALL *saints were flowery in their prayers. Blessed Rose Hawthorne Lathrop, daughter of the novelist Nathaniel Hawthorne, was both brief and pointed in her request for a* new home for members of her religious order, the Dominican Servants of Relief for Incurable Cancer.

Lord, You must give us this new house. We need it. And I have nobody to look to but You, dear Lord!

SAINT ANTHONY MARY CLARET

1807–1870

ONE WOULD *think that someone who preached more than ten thousand sermons, published two hundred books and pamphlets on Christianity, and confirmed more than one hundred thousand people would have few, if any, doubts about his faith. Yet Saint Anthony Mary Claret, founder of the Claretian Order and archbishop of Cuba, prayed not only for virtues such as goodness and chastity but also for the ability to believe more completely in the teachings of Christ.*

I believe, Lord, but let me believe more firmly.
I hope, Lord, but let me hope more surely.
I love, Lord, but let me love more warmly.
I repent, Lord, but let me repent more deeply.

❧

Father, give me humility, meekness, chastity,
    patience, and charity.

Father, teach me goodness, knowledge, and
discipline.
Father, give me your love together with your grace
and I will be rich enough.
My God, my Jesus, and my all.

SAINT PIERRE TOUSSAINT

1776–1863

A SLAVE *by birth and a hairdresser by trade, Saint Pierre Toussaint came to New York from his native Haiti just after the Revolutionary War. He was a man of remarkable humility, grace, and generosity; it was said of him that no finer gentleman ever walked the face of the earth.*

SAINT PIERRE'S DEATHBED PRAYER

God is with me, I want nothing on the earth.

BLESSED BROTHER ANDRÉ

1845–1937

URING *the fifty years he spent as a brother in the Congregation of the Holy Cross, Blessed Brother André worked innumerable miracles on behalf of the sick and dying. Sometimes called "The Miracle Worker of Montreal," he always attributed his cures not to his own prayers but to the intercession of Saint Joseph.*

O Holy Angels, grant that I may be filled with the presence of God on the altar as you are penetrated by it in Heaven.

BLESSED MARIE ROSE DUROCHER

1814–1849

A S A *young woman, Blessed Marie Rose Durocher longed to enter a convent, but ill health prevented her from doing so. She died not long after founding her own teaching order, the Sisters of the Holy Names of Jesus and Mary. Today her sisters are located throughout the world.*

DEATHBED PRAYER

My God, I cannot say, as Saint Teresa did: "To suffer or to die," but to suffer, O my God, and to do Your Will; behold, that is my desire! . . . Jesus, Mary, Joseph! Sweet Jesus, I love You. Jesus, be to me Jesus.

SAINT ROSE OF LIMA

1586–1617

S AINT ROSE OF LIMA *is the first canonized saint of the Americas. Born in Lima, Peru, she lived a life of severe self-mortification, penance, and prayer. She helped support her family by growing flowers and doing embroidery work, even after she dedicated her life to God as a member of the Third Order of Saint Dominic.*

Oh my God! who would not love You? Oh good Jesus! when will I begin to love You as I am obliged? How far am I from this perfect, intimate and generous love? Alas! I know not even how to love You. How shameful! What advantage is it to have a heart, unless it be quite consumed with love for You!

SAINT ANGELA MERICI OF BRESCIA

1474–1540

FOUNDRESS *of the oldest teaching order of women in the church, Saint Angela placed her sisters under the care of Saint Ursula; hence the name Ursulines. Although she experienced many mystical visions, she was also a practical and capable organizer and her prayer reflects her readiness to do God's will.*

O my God, speak, your servant is listening and is ready to obey you in all things.

SAINT JOHN BERCHMANS

1599–1621

"I F I DO NOT *become a saint when I am young, I shall never become one," said Saint John Berchmans. He got his desire, dying at age twenty-two. Like Saint Thérèse of Lisieux, he practiced "the little way" of faith, allowing daily life to be his penance. His simple prayer reflects his greatest desire.*

Lord, teach me how to pray. O Lord, in my meditation let a fire flame out. Open my lips, O Lord, and my mouth will declare Your praise.

SAINT JULIE BILLIART

1751–1816

WHILE *many saints have created their own prayers, many more have used the traditional words of the church. Saint Julie Billiart, the co-founder of the Institute of Notre Dame of Namur, prayed the Magnificat as she lay dying. Earlier in her life, she used the words of the following Act of Contrition to bring a dying woman peace.*

O my God, with all my heart I am sorry for having sinned against You, not because I fear the punishment my sins deserve, but because You are so good and because I owe to You everything good that I have ever had.

BLESSED MARGARET CLITHEROW

1556?–1586

"LET THEM *take all I have and save her, for she is the best wife in all England,"* begged Blessed Margaret Clitherow's husband at her trial for the crimes of harboring priests and attending Mass. His pleas were to no avail. Blessed Margaret was condemned to be crushed to death by a 700-pound weight. Her last words were "Jesus, have mercy on me!"*

God be thanked, all that He shall send me shall be welcome; I am not worthy of so good a death as this is: I have deserved death for my offenses to God, but not for anything that I am accused of.

SAINT ROSE PHILIPPINE DUCHESNE

1769–1852

*S*AINT ROSE PHILIPPINE DUCHESNE *was seventy-two before she realized her dream of becoming a missionary to the Native Americans. Although she never mastered the Potawatomi language, she was much loved by the people, who called her "The Woman Who Prays Always."*

You will go over the Jordan this day . . . say not in your heart, "for my justice has the Lord brought you to possess this land," take heed and beware, lest at any time you forget. . . . May God bless and confirm our resolution never to forget all that He has done for us.

SAINT JANE FRANCIS DE CHANTAL

1572–1641

S OME *friendships seem to be made in heaven—certainly that can be said of the friendship between Saint Jane Francis de Chantal and Saint Francis de Sales. Together they founded the Order of the Visitation, a community offering a spiritual way of life to women who were unsuited to the more severe ascetic orders. Saint Francis de Sales called Saint Jane Francis de Chantal "one of the holiest people I have ever met on this earth."*

Oh my God, if our souls seek You only and claim only Your love, why should we be displeased if our house is changed for us, since we carry You with us and find You in places wherever we go?

SAINT FRANCIS DE SALES

1567–1622

T HE BISHOP *of Geneva and a Doctor of the Church, Saint Francis de Sales was the author of numerous popular books and devotional manuals, the most famous of which is the* Introduction to the Devout Life. *Dedicating his life to teaching the way of sanctity to ordinary men and women, Saint Francis de Sales once said, "It is a mistake, a heresy, to want to exclude devoutness of life from among soldiers, from shops and offices, from royal courts, from the homes of the married."*

O God, may Your will be done, not only in the execution of Your commandments, counsels, and inspirations, which we ought to obey, but also in suffering the afflictions which befall us. May Your will be done in us and by us in everything that pleases You!

SAINT ALPHONSUS DE LIGUORI

1696–1787

S AINT ALPHONSUS DE LIGUORI, *an extremely successful lawyer, abandoned the law when he lost an important case. Entering religious life, he worked as a preacher in Naples and eventually founded his own religious order, the Redemptorists. Despite the fact he renounced his legal career, the erudition, logic, and keen use of language that served him at the bar is evident in his prayers.*

O God of love, do You, then, so much desire to dispense Your favors to us and yet are we so little anxious to obtain them? Oh, what sorrow we will feel at the hour of death, when we think of this negligence, so pernicious to our souls? O my Lord, forget, I beseech You, all that is past; for the future, with Your help, I will prepare myself better by endeavoring to detach my affections from everything that prevents me from receiving all those graces which You desire to give me.

Holy Spirit, divine Consoler, I adore you as my true
  God,
with God the Father and God the Son.
I adore you and unite myself to the adoration you
  receive from the angels and saints.
I give you my heart and I offer my ardent thanks-
  giving for all the grace which you never cease to
  bestow on me.

Eternal Father, your Son has promised that you would
grant all the graces we ask of you in his name. Trusting
in this promise, and in the name of and through the
merits of Jesus Christ, I ask of you five special graces:

First, I ask pardon for all the offenses I have com-
mitted, for which I am sorry with all my heart, because
I have offended your infinite goodness.

Second, I ask for your divine Light, which will enable me to see the vanity of all the things of this earth, and see also your infinite greatness and goodness.

Third, I ask for a share in your love, so that I can detach myself from all creatures, especially from myself, and love only your holy will.

Fourth, grant me the grace to have confidence in the merits of Jesus Christ and in the intercession of Mary.

Fifth, I ask for the grace of perseverance, knowing that whenever I call on you for assistance, you will answer my call and come to my aid;

I fear only that I will neglect to turn to you in time of need, and thus bring myself to ruin.

Grant me the grace to pray always, O Eternal Father, in the name of Jesus.

SAINT JOHN (DON) BOSCO

1815–1888

FILLED *with joie de vivre, Saint John Bosco worked tirelessly on behalf of poor, abandoned boys in his native Italy. As a young priest, one of his favorite sayings was "Enjoy yourself as much as you like. Just keep from sin." At the time of his death, his religious order, the Salesians, had nearly one thousand priests and nine hundred sisters. He said the following prayer when he was believed to be dying from pneumonia.*

Yes, Lord, if it please you, cure me. I will not refuse any work. If I can be of service to a few souls, grant, O Lord, by the intercession of Your most holy Mother, to return me to such health as will not be contrary to the welfare of my soul.

SAINT MAXIMILIAN KOLBE

1894–1941

W HEN *ten men were arbitrarily chosen to starve to death because of an attempted escape from the notorious death camp at Auschwitz, Saint Maximilian Kolbe stepped forward to take the place of one of them. Remarkably, the SS officer agreed. When the guards entered the "block of death" several days later, Saint Maximilian was still alive; in an act of severe mercy, the guards killed him with a shot of carbolic acid.*

Who would dare to imagine that You, oh infinite, eternal God, have loved me for centuries, or to be more precise, from before the beginning of the centuries?

In fact, you have loved me ever since you have existed as God; thus, you have always loved me and you shall always love me! . . .

Your love for me was already there, even when I had no existence, and precisely because You loved me, oh good God, You called me from nothingness to existence! . . .

For me you have created the skies scattered with stars, for me the earth, the seas, the mountains, the streams, and all the beautiful things on earth . . .

Still, this did not satisfy You; to show me close up that You loved me so tenderly, You came down from the purest delights of heaven to this tarnished and tear-ridden world, You lived amidst poverty, hard work and suffering; and finally, despised and mocked, You let yourself be suspended in torment on a vile scaffold between two criminals . . .

Oh God of love, You have redeemed me in this terrible though generous, fashion! . . .

Who would venture to imagine it?

BROTHER LAWRENCE

c. 1605–1691

ITTLE *is known about Brother Lawrence except that he was a solider and hermit before entering a Carmelite monastery in Paris. Although he spent most of his religious life as a kitchen worker, his* writings reveal his profound interior prayer life (and perhaps some of his struggles with monastic life).

Lord, I cannot do this unless You enable me.

SAINT ANSLEM

C. 1033–1109

A THEOLOGIAN, *scholar, and teacher, Saint Anslem was often embroiled in bitter battles with English kings over the rights of the church. Perhaps because so much of his life was full of strife, his prayers, like those of many other saints, beg God to be slow to anger and quick to forgive.*

My prayer is but a cold affair, Lord,
because my love burns with so small a flame,
but you who are rich in mercy
will not mete out to them your gifts
according to the dullness of my zeal,
but as your kindness is above all human love
so let your eagerness to hear
be greater than the feeling in my prayers.
Do this for them and with them, Lord,
so that they may speed according to your will
and thus ruled and protected by you,

always and everywhere,
may they come at last to glory and eternal rest,
through you who are living and reigning God,
through all ages.

๛

O Lord,
you are my Lord and my God,
yet I have never seen you.
You have created and redeemed me,
and have conferred on me all my good,
yet I know you not.
I was created in order that I might know you,
but I have not yet attained the goal of my creation.
I confess, O Lord,
and give you thanks,
that you have created me in your image,
so that I might be mindful of you
and contemplate you and love you.
I seek not to understand in order that I may believe;
rather, I believe in order that I may understand.

SAINT GREGORY NAZIANZUS

c. 330–390

ALTHOUGH *shy by nature, Saint Gregory Naz-
ianzus was an eloquent speaker and preacher.
He used his considerable talents to combat
the heresy of Arianism, which denied the divinity of Christ. It wasn't until the end of this life that
he was finally allowed to retire in solitude and contem-
plation.*

Alas, dear Christ, the Dragon is here again.

Alas, he is here: terror has seized me, and fear.

Alas that I ate of the fruit of the tree of knowledge.

Alas that his envy led me to envy too.

I did not become like God; I was cast out of Paradise.

Temper, sword, awhile, the heat of your flames

and let me go again about the garden,

entering with Christ, a thief from another tree.

SAINT LEO THE GREAT

400?–461

*S*AINT LEO THE GREAT *was pope when the barbarians were literally at the gates of Rome. In 452, Attila the Hun was ready to swarm over Italy, but Pope Leo persuaded him to back off. Three years later, when the Vandals arrived, Pope Leo was not so persuasive, but he did get them to agree not to burn Rome or slay its inhabitants, even though the city was completely sacked.*

Grant to us, O Lord, not to mind earthly things, but rather to love heavenly things, that while all things around us pass away, we even now may hold fast those things which last forever.

SAINT BRIDGID OF IRELAND

C. 452–524

ALTHOUGH *Bridgid is one of the most beloved Irish saints, the details of her life are lost to legend. Supposedly the daughter of a slave mother and a noble father, she is said to have* built the first convent in Ireland. Along with Saint Patrick, she is one of the patron saints of Ireland.

I would like the angels of Heaven to be among us.

I would like an abundance of peace.

I would like full vessels of charity.

I would like rich treasures of mercy.

I would like cheerfulness to preside over all.

I would like Jesus to be present.

I would like the three Marys of illustrious renown
to be with us.

I would like the friends of Heaven to be gathered
around us from all parts.

I would like myself to be a rent payer to the Lord;

that I should suffer distress, that he would bestow a good blessing upon me.

I would like a great lake of beer for the King of
Kings.
I would like to be watching Heaven's family drink-
ing it through all eternity.

SAINT PHILIP NERI

1515–1595

I F HAVING *a sense of humor were a criterion for entering heaven, Saint Philip Neri would be first in line. Bubbling over with mirth and lightheartedness, he said his favorite two books were the Bible and a jokebook. Although his short prayer has a jocular quality, it demonstrates the heartfelt desire for holiness that formed the basis of his life.*

O Jesus, watch over me always, especially today, or I shall betray you like Judas.

SAINT MECHTILDE OF MAGDEBURG

1210–C. 1285

A T LEAST *two famous women mystics named Mechtilde (or Mechtildis) lived at the famous convent of Helfta: Saint Mechtildis of Hackeborn-Wippra, who was responsible for the upbringing of Saint Gertrude the Great, and Saint Mechtilde of Magdeburg, the author of this prayer. Saint Mechtilde of Magdeburg was an ascetic whose intense prayer life resulted in several heavenly visions. This prayer, however, reflects a humble woman who was willing to offer up her all-too-earthly blindness.*

Lord, I thank you that in your love you have taken from me all earthly riches, and that you now clothe and feed me through the kindness of others. Lord, I thank you, that since you have taken from me the sight of my eyes, you serve me now with the eyes of others.

Lord, I thank you that since you have taken away the power of my hands and my heart, you serve me by the hands and hearts of others. Lord, I pray for them. Reward them for it in your heavenly love, that they may faithfully serve and please you till they reach a happy end.

SAINT THOMAS AQUINAS

1225–1274

ONE OF *the greatest minds the Western world has ever produced, the Dominican friar Saint Thomas Aquinas is a key figure in the development of Christian theology. Called "The Dumb Ox" by his classmates in Paris, Saint Thomas is the author of the greatest single work on faith ever written, the* Summa Theologiae. *His prayers are among the most well known of those written by the saints.*

PRAYER BEFORE STUDY OR READING

Grant to me, O merciful God, that I might ardently
   love,
prudently ponder,
rightly acknowledge,
and perfectly fulfill all that is pleasing to you,
   for the praise and glory of your Name.

PRAYER BEFORE LECTURING,
WRITING OR PREACHING

Ineffable Creator, from the treasure house of your Wisdom you have created the three Angelic Hierarchies. In marvelous order you established them above the Empyrean Heaven, and splendidly arranged all the parts of creation.

I ask you, true Fountain of Light and Wisdom, the only creator of all things, to mercifully pour forth into my shadowed understanding the radiance of your love, that it might purge the twofold darkness of sin and ignorance into which I was born.

You, who have given voice to the tongues of infants, instruct my tongue also, and pour forth the grace of your blessing onto my lips.

Grant me prompt understanding, sure memory, direct and easy comprehension, insightful interpretation, and graciousness in speaking.

Launch, O Jesus, my beginning, guide my progress, and let my end be only yourself, who are true God and true Man, living and reigning through all the ages of ages. Amen.

❧

Oversee, O my God, my life, that I might do what you ask of me; allow me to see and permit me to do whatever is fitting and profitable to my soul.

Lead me not, O Lord my God, into excessive wealth or want, lest I put my trust in riches, or despair in misery.

Let me take no joy or sorrow, save in what would lead me to you or from you. Let me delight only in pleasing you and fear only displeasing you.

O Lord, let all passing things seem worthless to me and let everything eternal become my treasure. May I despise any joy apart from you and seek nothing that is

without you. Make carrying burdens for you my relax-
ation, O Lord, and rest without you itself a burden.

> Cross, my certain salvation,
> Cross, whom I ever adore,
> Cross of the Lord be with me,
> Cross, my refuge, forever more.

SAINT CATHERINE DEI RICCI

1522–1590

S AINT CATHERINE DEI RICCI, *an Italian visionary, relived the passion of Christ each week from noon on Thursday until 4:00 P.M. on Friday for twelve years. She was accustomed to saying this prayer each Friday shortly before retiring.*

My friends and my neighbors
have drawn near and stood against me.
  (Ps. 38 [37]:12)
I was delivered up, and came not forth:
my eyes languished through poverty.
  (Ps .88 [87]:9–10)
And his sweat came down as drops of blood,
trickling on the ground. *(Lk. 22:44)*
For many dogs have encompassed me,
the council of the malignant has besieged me.
  (Ps. 22[21]:17)

I have given my body to the strikers
and my cheeks to them that plucked them.
  (Is. 50:6a)
I have not turned my face from them that rebuked
  me,
and spit upon me. *(Is. 50:6b)*
For I am ready for scourges,
and my sorrow is continually before me.
  (Ps. 39 [38]:18)
And pleating a crown of thorns,
they put it on his head. *(Mt. 27:29)*
They have pierced my hands and my feet;
they have numbered all my bones. *(Ps. 22 [21]:18)*
And they gave me gall for my food,
and in my thirst they gave me vinegar to drink.
  (Ps. 69[68]:22)

All they that saw me have laughed me to scorn;
they have spoken with the lips and wagged the
head. *(Ps. 22[21]:8)*
They have looked and stared upon me.
They have parted my garments amongst them;
and upon my vesture they have cast lots.
(Ps. 22 [21]:18b–19)
Into your hands I commend my spirit:
you have redeemed me, O Lord, the God of truth.
(Ps. 31[30]:6)
Look, we beg you, O Lord, upon this your house-
hold for whom
Our Lord Jesus Christ did not hesitate to give himself over into the hands of sinners and undergo
the torment of the Cross.

SAINT VINCENT FERRER

c. 1350–1419

F AMOUS *as a preacher, Saint Vincent Ferrer traveled through much of Western Europe, attracting huge crowds wherever he went. This petition is part of a longer prayer asking for a happy and holy death.*

O Lord, since, many different dangers and temptations may occur, should it happen (God forbid) that through them I deviate from that Holy Faith, either at the time of death or some other confusion of mind, or should I consent to any sin, I make profession of it here and now before your Most Holy Majesty, and in the presence of your most glorious mother Mary, my Guardian Angel, my Holy Father Dominic, and all the saints.

SAINT JOHN OF THE CROSS

1542–1591

S AINT JOHN OF THE CROSS, *author of* Dark Night of the Soul, *was a close friend of another great saint, Teresa of Avila. A poet as well as a theologian, mystic, and reformer of the Carmelite Order, he was misunderstood and misinterpreted even by members of his own order. He bore the marks of the beatings he received at the order of the vicar general of the Carmelites until his death.*

Pull me from this death,
my God, and give me Life.
Do not hold me so tightly
in this knot.
See how I long to see you;
my affliction is so complete.
If only I could die
because then I would not die.

SAINT STEPHEN

FIRST CENTURY A.D.

THE DEATH of Saint Stephen, the first Christian martyr, is recorded in the Acts of the Apostles. According to the account, he was stoned to death by a band of zealots led by a young man named Saul, one day to be known as Saint Paul. As he was dying, Saint Stephen, like Jesus, asked God to forgive his attackers.

Lord Jesus, receive my spirit!

SAINT POLYCARP

c. 69–c. 155

*S*HORTLY *after returning to Smyrna from Rome, where he had been helping to set the date for Easter, elderly Saint Polycarp was burned alive when he refused to recant his faith. His prayer, modeled after those that he would have said each Sunday during the liturgical services, is one of the oldest prayers of the Church.*

O Lord God Almighty, Father of your blessed and beloved son Jesus Christ, though whom we have been given knowledge of you; You are the God of angels and powers, of the whole creation, and of all the generations of the righteous who live in your sight. I bless you for granting me this day and hour, that I may be numbered among the martyrs, to share the cup of your Anointed and to rise again to life everlasting, both in body and soul, in the immortality of the Holy Spirit. May I be received among them this day in your presence, a sacrifice rich and acceptable, even as you did appoint and fore-show, and now bring to pass, for you are the God of truth and in you there is no falsehood. For this, and for all else besides, I praise you, I bless you, I glorify you through our eternal High Priest in heaven, your beloved son Jesus Christ, by whom and with whom be glory to you and the Holy Spirit, now and for all ages to come.

SAINT THOMAS MORE

1478–1535

Immortalized *as "A Man for All Seasons," Saint Thomas More was lord chancellor of England under King Henry VIII. Because of his opposition to Henry's divorce from Catherine of Aragon and subsequent marriage to Anne Boleyn, Saint Thomas was imprisoned for a year in the Tower of London before finally being beheaded. At his death he announced, "I die the King's good servant, but God's first."*

On Behalf of an Enemy
Almighty God, have mercy on *(Name)*
and on all that bear me evil will and would do me
    harm,
and on their faults and mine together.
By such easy, tender, merciful means as your own
    infinite wisdom can best devise;
vouchsafe to amend and redress and make us saved
    souls in heaven together.

Where we may ever live and love together with you and your blessed saints.

A GODLY MEDITATION

Written in the Tower of London
a year before he was beheaded

Give me your grace, good Lord, to set the world at nought,
to set my mind fast upon you and not to hang upon the blast of men's mouths.
To be content to be solitary.
Not to long for worldly company,
little and little utterly to cast off the world, and rid my mind of the business thereof.
Not to long to hear of any worldly things,

But that the hearing of worldly fantasies may be to
    me displeasant.
Gladly to be thinking of God,
busily to labor to love him.
To know my own vility and wretchedness,
to humble and meeken myself under the mighty
    hand of God,
To bewail my sins passed;
For the purging of them, patiently to suffer
    adversity.
Gladly to bear my purgatory here,
to be joyful of tribulations,
to walk the narrow way that leads to life.
To bear the cross with Christ,
to have the last thing—death—in remembrance,
to have ever before my eye death, that is ever at
    hand;
To make death no stranger to me;
to foresee and consider the everlasting fire of hell;
To pray for pardon before the Judge comes.

To have continually in mind the passion that Christ
    suffered for me;
for his benefits uncessantly to give him thanks,
to buy the time gain that I before have lost.
To abstain from vain confabulations,
to eschew light foolish mirth and gladness;
To cut off unnecessary recreations.
Of worldly substance, friends, liberty, life and all—
to set the loss at nought for the winning of Christ.
To think my worst enemies my best friends,
for the brethren of Joseph could never have done
    him so much good
with their love and favor as they did him with their
    malice and hatred.

THOMAS Á KEMPIS

c. 1380–1471

BEST *known as the author of the* Imitation of Christ, *Thomas á Kempis took as his motto, "Everywhere I have sought rest and found it nowhere, save in tiny nooks with tiny books." His writings include sermons, lives of the saints, and devotional materials. His prayer is a masterpiece of simplicity and humility.*

> O Lord God, holy Father, be you now and forever blessed.
> For as you will, so it has been done; and what you do is good.
> Let your servant rejoice in you,
> not in myself or any other.
> You alone are my hope and my crown.
> You are my goodness and my honor.

O Lord, what does your servant have but what has
   been received from you
without deserving it?
Yours are all things that you have been given and
   have made.

SAINT MARGARET MARY ALACOQUE

1647–1690

SAINT MARGARET MARY ALACOQUE *saw a vision of Jesus in which his heart was visible and surrounded by thorns and flames. Because of her dedication to the Sacred Heart of Jesus, as the image became known, she established the devotion of the Sacred Heart throughout much of the Catholic Church.*

O Heart of Love,
I put all my trust in you.
For I fear all things from my own weakness,
but I hope for all things from your goodness.

Had I thousand bodies, O my God, a thousand loves and a thousand lives, I would immolate them all to Your service.

SAINT JOHN EUDES

1601–1680

S AINT JOHN EUDES *is especially remembered for three things: first, for caring for victims of the Plague; second, for establishing rehabilitation homes for former prostitutes; and third, for helping to spread the devotion of the Sacred Heart of Jesus. His prayer for a special favor is one all Christians can relate to.*

O desire of my soul, grant me the favor I implore;
hearken to the cry of my heart.
You know, O Lord, what I ask of you;
My heart has so often told you.

SAINT LUTGARDE OF AYWIERES

1182–1246

S AINT LUTGARDE *of Aywieres was a Cistercian sister with gifts of prophecy and healing. A contemporary of Saint Francis and the first recorded stigmatic, she was also a pioneer in the devotion to the Sacred Heart of Jesus.*

Take my heart dear Lord. May your heart's love be so mingled and united with my heart that I may possess my heart in you. May it ever remain there safe in your protection.

SAINT BERNARD OF CLAIRVAUX

1090–1153

S AINT BERNARD *of Clairvaux was sometimes said to be willful and hard, but he was the most severe on himself. His stern ascetic nature caused him serious health problems, but his mystical nature and devotional writings have influenced thousands. His prayers reflect his utter dependence on Christ for strength and guidance.*

Oh, how good and pleasant a thing it is to dwell in
the Heart of Jesus!
Who is there that does not love a heart so wounded?
Who can refuse a return of love to a heart so loving?

Come Lord Jesus,
take away scandals from Your kingdom which is my
soul,
and reign there.
You alone have the right.

For greediness comes to claim a throne within me;
haughtiness and self-assertion would rule over me;
pride would be my king;
luxury says, "I will reign";
ambition, detraction, envy and anger struggle
within me for the mastery.
I resist as far as I am able;
I struggle according as help is given me.
I call on my Lord Jesus.
For his sake I defend myself,
since I acknowledge myself as wholly his possession.
He is my God,
Him I proclaim my Lord.
I have no other king than my Lord, Jesus Christ.
Come, then, O Lord, and disperse these enemies by
your power,
and you shall reign in me, for you are my King and
my God.

SAINT MARY MAGDALEN DEI PAZZI

1566–1607

A CARMELITE *mystic and native of Florence, Saint Mary Magdalen dei Pazzi was a pious child, dedicating herself to God at age ten. After entering the Carmelite convent, she experienced numerous episodes of both mystical experiences and intense suffering, but her prayer is one of peace and calm.*

Spirit of truth,
you are the reward to the saints,
the comforter of souls,
light in the darkness,
riches to the poor,
treasure to lovers,
food for the hungry,
comfort to the wanderer;
to sum up,
you are the one in whom all treasures are contained.

SAINT EDMUND

1170–1240

SAINT EDMUND *of Abingdon, archbishop of Canterbury, was a scholar, preacher, and teacher at both Oxford and Paris. Known for his holiness and austerity, he spent much of his life in disagreement with King Henry III over foreign affairs. His prayer is a clear example of a Morning Offering.*

Into your hands, O Lord,
and into the hands of your holy angels,
I commit and entrust this day my soul,
my relations, my benefactors, my friends and my
    enemies,
and all your people.
Keep us, O Lord, through this day
by the merits and intercession of the Blessed Virgin
    Mary and all the saints.

SAINT JOHN CHRYOSTOM

c. 347–407

*S*AINT JOHN'S *sermons were so brilliant he was given the title Chryostom, or "Golden-mouthed." Not everyone loved his preaching, however. The Empress Eudoxia took personal umbrage at his denouncement of luxury and extravagance in the court and had him banished to the Taurus Mountains. In ill health and forced to travel in bad weather, he died on his way to the Black Sea.*

Almighty God, who has given us grace at this time with one accord to make our common supplication to you, and has promised through your well-beloved Son that when two or three are gathered in his name you will be in the midst of them: Fulfill now, O Lord, the desires and petitions of your servants as may be best for us; granting in this world knowledge of your truth and in the world to come life everlasting.

We give thanks to God that we have not sown our seed upon rocks, nor dropped it amid thorns; and that we have neither needed much time, nor long delay, in order that we might reap the harvest.

BLESSED MIGUEL PRO

1891–1927

A priest in Mexico during a time when being a priest was a crime, Blessed Miguel was betrayed by a young boy. Sentenced to be shot, he asked only that he be allowed to spend a few minutes in prayer before his execution and to die with his arms outstretched in the shape of a cross. His dying words, "Long live Christ the King," resonate with all who live and die for their faith.

O Lord, your empty tabernacles mourn
while we alone upon our Calvary
as orphans, ask you, Jesus to return
and dwell again within your sanctuary . . .
O Lord, why has your presence from us fled?
Do you not remember how in days gone by
those countless hearts which in their trials bled
found comfort in the light that from you shone? . . .
By the bitter tears of those who mourn their dead,

by our martyrs' blood for you shed joyfully,
by the crimson stream with which your heart has
  bled,
returning haste to your dear sanctuary.

SAINT CLEMENT OF ROME

A.D. 99

AUTHOR *of the* First Epistle of Clement, *one of the most important writings of the early church, Saint Clement was the third pope of the Catholic Church.*

We beseech you O Lord, to grant us your help and protection.

Deliver the afflicted, pity the lowly, raise the fallen, reveal yourself to the needy, heal the sick, and bring home your wandering people. Feed the hungry, ransom the captive, support the weak, comfort the fainthearted. Let all the nations of the earth know that you alone are God, that Jesus Christ is your child and that we are your people and the sheep of your pasture.

SAINT FRANCES CABRINI

1850–1917

T HE FIRST *United States citizen to be canonized, Saint Frances Cabrini arrived from Italy in 1889. She immediately devoted herself to the influx of Italian immigrants, working tirelessly building schools, orphanages, and hospitals. At the opening of her first orphanage, she found a loaf of fresh-baked bread at the foot of a statue of Jesus, and she responded with this prayer.*

Bread of Heaven,
Bread of Love,
Bread of Life
shall never be lacking from God's little orphaned
children

SAINT HILDEGARD OF BINGEN

1098–1179

S AINT HILDEGARD, *German mystic and abbess, inspired even such famous saints as Bernard of Clairvaux. Her collection of mystical visions, called the* Scivias, *focuses on the relationship between God and humanity. In addition to her sacred writings, she also composed hymns, wrote plays, advised priests and the laity, and ran her monastery at Bingen.*

O budded, greening branch!
You stand as firmly rooted in your nobility
As the dawn advances.
Now rejoice and be glad;
Consider us frail ones worthy
To free us from our destructive ways:
Put forth your hand and
Raise us up.

SAINT CATHERINE OF GENOA

1447–1510

WHILE *being a mystic is difficult under ordinary circumstances, being a mystic while married to an unfaithful spendthrift with a nasty temper would seem to be almost impossible. Yet Saint Catherine of Genoa achieved the nearly impossible. Ultimately, her devotion converted her husband, and together they worked for twenty years serving the poor and sick.*

O tender Love, I want all of you. I could not live if I thought I were to do without even a spark of you.

SAINT CYRIL

A.D. 444

S EVERAL *men named Cyril have become saints,
but the most famous—and the one who is most
likely the author of this prayer—is Saint Cyril of
Alexandria. A Doctor of the Church and archbishop of Alexandria, he had a great devotion to the
Eucharist.*

O God of love, who has given a new commandment
through your only begotten son, that we should love
one another, even as you love us, the unworthy and the
wandering, and gave your beloved son for our life and
salvation. We pray, O Lord, that you give to us, your
servants, in all time of our life on earth, a mind which
forgets past ill-will, a pure conscience, sincere thoughts
and a heart to love our brethren.

SAINT DIMITRII OF ROSTOV

SEVENTEENTH CENTURY

A RENOWNED *bishop and preacher, Saint Dimitrii was much loved by the people he served. Although not widely known in the West, his writings are greatly respected, especially by members of the Russian Orthodox Church.*

Come, my Light, and illumine my darkness.

Come, my Life, and revive me from death.

Come, my Physician, and heal my wounds.

Come, Flame of divine love, and burn up the thorns
of my sins, kindling my heart with the flame of
your love.

Come, my King, sit upon the throne of my heart
and reign there.

For you alone are my King and my Lord.

BLESSED JORDAN OF SAXONY

A.D. 1237

ALL SAINTS *pray to God, but many saints also ask the intercession of their fellow men and women on the journey to heaven. Blessed Jordan of Saxony, the second master general of the Dominican order, prayed this prayer to his mentor Saint Dominic.*

O most holy priest of God, faithful confessor, and noble preacher, Saint Dominic, man chosen by the Lord, beloved and in your life pleasing to God above all others; glorious for your life, teaching, and miracles, we rejoice to have you as our gracious advocate before God. I cry out to you, whom I honor with special devotion among the saints and elect of God, in this valley of sorrow. Be compassionately present, I ask, to my sinsick soul bereft of every virtue and grace, bound as it is by so many vices and the stain of so many sins. Be present to my wretched and unhappy soul, O blessed and happy soul of the man of God, whom Divine Grace endowed with such blessings that you not only achieved a place of happy rest, blessed refreshment, and heavenly glory for yourself, but also drew numberless others to the same beatitude through your sweet admonition, fervent preaching, and praise-worthy life. Attend then, O Blessed Dominic, and lend a compassionate ear to my voice in supplication . . .

INDEX